Old News

poems by

James Broschart

Finishing Line Press
Georgetown, Kentucky

Old News

ACKNOWLEDGMENTS

Grateful thanks are due to editors of publications where some of these poems first
appeared.

"Growing Season" in *Ars Medica*, v.4, n.1

"Hometown" within "The North Branch" in *Blueline* v.30

"Patchwork" in *Artemis* 14

"Castaway" in *Artemis* 16

"Father's Day" in *The Enigmatist* 2008

I would also like to express my appreciation to the members of our local poetry workshop,
meeting regularly every two weeks or so for over ten years. These friends and fellow
poets have seen and critiqued at one time or another all of the poems in this collection.
Consequently all of them have had a hand in bringing my poems to completion. I cannot
adequately express my gratitude to each and every one of you.

Publisher: Leah Maines

Editor: Christen Kincaid

Cover Art: *Self Portrait,* James Broschart

Author Photo: Jennifer Broschart

Cover Design: Elizabeth Maines McCleavy

Printed in the USA on acid-free paper.
Order online: www.finishinglinepress.com
                    also available on amazon.com

Author inquiries and mail orders:
Finishing Line Press
P. O. Box 1626
Georgetown, Kentucky 40324
U. S. A.

Table of Contents

This is for Kay, who puts up with my distraction.

Pie

Dad would scoop and eat his filling first,
then the crust. Mom shuddered,
said it was common. He laughed,
said he liked the taste that way.
Besides, her crust was the best part.

Mom tried to get him to sit up
straight, move his elbows,
take off his hat. Set an example.

He finally agreed to the hat,
but claimed the rest got in the way
of eating, and eating was why
they were sitting there, wasn't it?

My mother carried on like this
a lot when I was young,
notions I thought I'd outgrown
until I heard them from my own lips.
I try for Dad, get Mom instead.

Echoes

My wife clicks on a retro music station
as I struggle with the fine print in my newspaper.
Startled, I recognize the strident beat
of tunes not heard since our kids departed.

They left behind fading artwork on the fridge
and all those growth marks that climb the doorframe
into the kitchen, where a table with extra chairs
offers up meals too large for just the two of us.

Now we take infrequent trips to their distant homes,
where our still uncertain role as grandparents
confounds our sleep and makes us uneasy guests,
amid family scenes we scarcely recognize.

Our own rooms grow dusty and unused
in a house where echoes substitute for laughter
and the clatter of running feet on the stairs
has been replaced by the slap of ragged slippers.

Coca-Cola, 1948

The Johnson sisters sit on their front porch,
observe the neighbors and gossip boldly.
Their raucous voices and piercing laughter
fill Second Street from Pine to Poplar.

Both blowsy blondes of mysterious ages
wear billowing muumuus dotted with posies.
Their painted toenails stick over the edges
of matching pink scuffs as they rock and yak.

I was their ten year-old fetch and carry boy,
hired to keep them supplied with Coca-Cola
I lug from the corner store two blocks over.
That's where I hustle with a carton of empties

every afternoon, clutching six nickels
plus one to squander on jawbreakers or taffy
from glass jars waiting behind a winking
Table Queen Bread Girl on the store's screen door.

I butler their glasses with fresh ice cubes
cracked loose from a dented Frigidaire tray,
then pour out the Coke, careful not to foam over,
leaving the full inch of empty they want.

They keep a pint in a brown paper bag
they think well hidden behind the begonias,
but I'd seen them top off enough to suspect
high-test Coke is what fuels their devotions.

I know not to linger or listen too closely
to their meaty language and rowdy jokes
but I learn a lot to try on my playmates
when I slip off the porch and scoot toward home.

Kinetic Energy

Spring! Tightly-coiled kids
erupt from their houses
reclaim their old bikes
pop wheelies and race
to check out the creek,

then run, run, run
in mud-soaked sneakers,
build forts in vacant lots
and play cops and robbers
or aliens attacking the Earth,

until the light begins to fail
when they pretend not to hear
parents calling them home
from games like Red Rover
and Capture the Flag.

Satisfaction

This day went well.
I worked in the yard,
weeding, clearing brush,

staking once-dull stalks
transformed with green tips
and a mist of early blossoms.

Bees appeared
to scold my location
each time I moved.

I stacked branches
and tried to outwit the dog
as he stole sticks from the pile.

We both survived these encounters
and were deeply satisfied. Tomorrow
I'd like another day like this.

Growing Season

Rodney,
master gardener and noted urologist,
gloves his hands and places the plough
into the field between my parted legs.

David,
tall, dark, distinguished radiation oncologist,
did not plan to become a farmer in his prime,
yet plants the seeds methodically into my gland.

Together
these scientists admire their handiwork:
rows and furrows laid, aiming toward a harvest
meant only to yield barren ground.

In the Park

Old men shift on hard stone benches
and hope the sun will do its best.
They brag about their surgeries
as though body parts were trophies.

Coveys of shirt-sleeved deskmen
flock pavements to stand and preen.
Some chuff loudly into cell phones
or eye crowds grazing food carts.

Young mothers airing infants meet,
block walkways with their strollers;
in low voices they plan ways
to organize the world. Joggers jink

to dodge small children, who shriek
and scramble over two lovers lying
tight together on the grass,
wishing for solitude.

Drifter

An old house slumps
weatherworn and faded
by the side of the highway,

hard used by a lifetime of travel
from the open countryside
to this crowded thoroughfare.

Barely clad in the tatters
of something once fashionable
it stands hipshot and weary,

as though flagging down cars
to try for a lift
all the way through to the coast.

On the Appearance of Wing Flashing in the Northern Mockingbird

Science studies and surmises,
focuses on your sex life,
marks your urge to strut
and dare the reckless intruder,
or reckons you flush out insect prey
by your two-step incantation.

Yet these easy mechanistic answers
do not fit your fey embrace;
you, so rarely silent, rough and rowdy,
so filled with life's pent energies,
do raise your wings thus to reveal
some brief glimpse of inner grace.

Value System

What is worthwhile? A sunset,
where the sky flaunts color
and deepening hue.

Early morning stillness
when it fills us
with anticipation.

The longing for movement
that comes upon us
when we lie down together
and touch.

The lurch of the heart
when someone's child
takes a first step.

This world,
when we remember
that we are guests.

Rhythm

I'd long embraced my heart alone
to mark my life, as metronome;
it measured out, and that was all.

But then I felt your footfall:
growing louder, to interrupt my pace,
seizing onto rhythm. I faced

you, and yielded to your glance,
giving up my heartbeat
to our insistent dance.

Warrior

for Kay

Like an Amazon she yielded up her breast without hesitation,
having already sacrificed her abdomen to cruel therapies
and been assured twice over that she was as near to cured
as could be found to fit the scope of scientific knowledge.

Her body is now a landscape of treatment histories,
a map of the battlefield she has so far won,
though it still displays regions as yet uncharted
where oncology's cartographers plead ignorance.

Weary, this veteran warrior must stand ready
and never relax the vigilance of her guard.
Each new day completed means the truce is holding.
Every night reminds her there is no armistice.

Fashion Statement

Don't care
what clothes you wear,
which shoes, what style your hair.
Your smile, your glance, just you so fair,
suits me.

Curriculum

Love has its own arithmetic
where one plus one is always greater,
though sometimes, sadly, we shape
its geometry from triangles.

Love also has a grammar, with
the second person favored first,
and *thou* replaces *I* and *me*
in thoughts and declarations.

Love's language is often learned unspoken:
meanings transmitted by tilt of head
or accomplished through the eyes,
whose glance can fill a dictionary.

Love's history lectures may be unique
and its future lesson-plans a mystery,
but both yield to the present moment,
where Love becomes our social science.

Love's geography is our favorite subject,
even though that homework is never finished.

June Moon

Would June have gotten such a boost
when paired with Moon, had this induced
a swarm of creatures loose at night
and dead arisen, taking flight?

October's moon is no less bright
yet passion frowns on its bleak light,
instead this shining orb is blamed
for frights so dire they can't be named.

If star-crossed lovers will insist
on moonlit nights to make their tryst
then for their comfort, ease, and calm
they must be set a month that's warm.

Thus June's sweet moon serves love full time
and submits, with grace, to doggerel rhyme.

Social Contract

The photographer rearranges us,
confident in his power
to make or break our memories.

Bride and groom stand rictus-faced,
unsteady in their long poses,
perhaps a foreshadowing.

It's time to witness their clumsy
coupling to cut the cake,
ravish each other's mouth.

We search for place cards amid
hasty trading, inspect with suspicion
plates offered by some unknown chef,

skew our chairs to shift uneasily
through speeches filled with
inside jokes in bad taste.

We pony up for our second drinks,
shout to be heard, attempt to dance
only to be halted on command

to freeze and smile
for each blinding flash of light—
Twister in fancy dress.

Those of us not used to moving
sit hard to catch our breaths,
until the master of ceremonies

thinks of more embarrassments
for the crowd to perform,
to be treasured in the telling.

Crescent Beach

I walk the bright white crescent
of morning beach again,
amid the crowds going and coming,
striding, jogging, overtaking.

All intent: some still pale, newly arrived;
some showing the vivid blush
of their passionate pursuit;
some darkened veterans
of the chase to win the sun.

The hard-packed rim of tidal sand
at water's edge is a narrow track,
where shoulders brush, positions pass
to those who set a firmer pace.

Some step away, discover
deeper footing, harder going.
Yet here and there someone's paused
to pick a shell,
or watch a wading bird.

I've been one of those who hesitate,
less interested in the horizon
than what lies beneath my feet.
What I've found I carry with me still.

I strike across these furrows now,
heading in, my walking done,
my aim fixed toward the place
where we once started out.

My eyes still smart
from the sun's crisp glare,
or is it from the memory
of our children digging there
in this clean white sand;

of our days upon this beach,
a young family, newly risen,
preparing to face together
the bright intensity?

Growth Chart

We made our marks on this door's frame,
each one of us pressed tight, heads back,
better postures than we ever usually managed.
Every line was drawn by someone else
in vain hope of preventing exaggeration.

Those dates and names signify
our flood stages, from child to teen.
That lowest line is for Eleanor,
a dog remembered as taller and wiser
than her mark might indicate.

Me? I'm still at it, though I appear
to be growing shorter every year.
I'm sure there's a mistake in my method.
Would you be so kind?
There's a pencil hanging from that string.

The Year Our Son Disappeared

into his room we hardly noticed.
After all, we still had a daughter
who wanted to go shopping
on days she wasn't begging for a pony.

We knew he was still somewhere
in the house, since every morning
empty milk cartons appeared
on the kitchen table.

I bumped into someone in the hallway
outside the bathroom door once,
whose strange deep voice
reminded me of him.

Maybe if we paste an old photo
onto one of those milk cartons
we might get word.

Dogs

what do dogs dream?
legs churn while tails beat the floor
nothing can escape

Life With Dogs

First of all, they'll eat anything—
anything—
and then lick anywhere,
just before they want
to lick you.

And the barking! Don't
get me started on the barking.
You may as well
stop the paper,
and open a post office box.

But they'll want to come
in the car to the post office,
still barking.
Just try to clean that spit
from the windows.

And the mud! Forget about
restoring the oriental.
Plus, they jump onto your bed
very early every morning,
and love you to death.

My Grandson

runs through the house
for the sheer delight of it,
on legs so recently mastered
his stops and turns
become achievements
or near tragedies.

Falling is still the experience
he's most accomplished at,
and his grace provides a glimpse
into his future
as he comes up laughing
most times, ready for more.

That top shelf is a peak
waiting to be conquered,
and he looks it over every day.
Unknown to us he already
has his base camp selected
on the arm of the nearby sofa.

He teeters out from it to grab
at—*whoops*—the next shelf
down
but I manage just in time
to haul him in,
already tensed for the next assault.

Generation Gap

I spent some time putting up the tent
while my grandson watched from the window,
between games on his PlayStation.

"Surprise me," he'd said when I asked
if he wanted to help. I could see
my work was cut out for me.

I knew he could find other worlds within that tent
if only he'd give it a chance. A castle, a fighter
plane, a pirate ship: all were there under the canvas.

My son, preparing to manicure his lawn,
took the tent down the next day,
relieved it hadn't yellowed the grass.

Encounter

I see two boys coming down the lane,
talking, walking, bumping together as boys do;
interrupting each other with excited declarations
and shrill assertions and emphatic repetitions,
laughing and crowing, sometimes pushing,
all the while smiling, nodding,
gesturing agreements and understandings.

They lean together comfortably, unselfconsciously,
as though to underscore some like-minded meaning.
Their hands touch.
They look quickly at one another out of the corners of their eyes.
They smile.

And, just as I had raised my hand to hail them,
to say "Hello," to say "How's it going boys," they see me:
and step apart,
look down,
walk sedately;
make no notice of my outstretched hand.

Recollection

My wallet is a tomb
for a history
hardly remembered.

A cache of battered cards
hawk services once sought.
Creased scraps of paper
hint at orphaned names

to puzzle over.
Illegible phone numbers
disclose a web
of lost entanglements.

Frayed photographs captured
by methods no longer used
exhibit faces now no longer young,
faded scenes of places all but forgotten.

A driver's license that may be expired
bears an image scarcely visible
behind the cataract of its window.

Memories shy away
despite these aging prompts,
uneasy at the edges
of my remaining presence.

Family Bulletin

The news of the day
has nothing to do
with results of the election
or the threat from abroad.
Instead,
has the dog been out?
Did you pick up your room?
Has Dad found work?
Anyone heard from Sissy?
Is Nana still breathing?

Castaway

Uncle Fred stares at nothing near,
speaks in a liquid rasp hardly heard
over the hiss of his oxygen.

He whispers old memories
of crashing seas and a blue so bright
it could burn your eyes,

of iron hulls that carried him
on the trackless paths of oceans
scrubbing the sands of far-off shores.

My father, restless for a smoke,
turns to go out as I sit and dream,
lost in a kid's imagination.

Fred's voice swirls and sighs
like a shell held tight against my ear
while I strain to hear the distant surf.

He struggles to regain the surface,
sucking for air as he reaches out
for one more tale to moor us.

I hear the ebb and flow of his wet gasp
and wonder if that restless sea
will drown him in his sleep.

Sometimes When I Forget to Breathe,

I'll hesitate,
hoping to discover why
my body is reluctant
to continue with the dance
whose steps I learned so long ago,

before the music faded and the rhythm
lost its ceaseless pull on my imagination.

Then,
as I take the next insistent breath
whose shudder is so disquieting,
to restart the habit of a lifetime
and cover up my lapse of continuity,

I know that soon enough,
at a time not of my choosing,
I'll forget to breathe again.

In the Land of Old Men

we pee in small jars, wait
patiently for someone to probe
a vein; we take deep breaths,
turn our heads and cough,
bend over.

In the land of old men we play
musical chairs in waiting rooms,
mention medications
we've seen on TV,
make follow-up appointments.

We live in a land with a blurred horizon
and plan our outings for daylit hours.
We drive in the middle lane,
keep a lookout for a place to stop
and hope for a clean restroom.

In the land of old men we eat early,
wait for parking by the entrance,
choose the house salad
instead of fries, sip iced tea
and long for something stronger.

We shop for looser sizes and tell
the clerk to please speak up.
We cover our purple spiderweb legs
and hide those grapefruit-colored
bruises that always seem to linger on.

We count our pills like rosary beads,
read the obituaries before the headlines,
mark our calendars for a service at ten
on Wednesday, where in lieu of flowers
we'll go to see who's still here.

Aoede

Ask the goddess for music
and she will laugh
but it will be a song.

Surface Tension

His path to grace won't be his face, I fear;
no noble brow nor Roman prow lives there.
And while his ears would sooner suit a jug,
at least they match, and balance out his mug.

What hair's his own, while fair, so lank and thin
it fails to hide the shine, or mask his chin;
a pity since his jaw needs much more thrust
to help his smile, spread 'cross his dial, win trust.

His specs so dense I can't make sense, you see,
where he is aimed—I must suppose it's me.
I'm puzzled why he'd catch my eye; you'd think
I'd spurn away his offer of a drink.

Yet, what you see is never what you get:
turned out to be the finest man I've met.
I took a chance and put aside my pride,
looked past his face, and saw the grace inside.

Quid Pro Crow

The sheep, snugged tight against cool stone,
discuss the field and fault its flavor.
A yard so bare pulls crows alone—
the plough's turned worms, and buried clover.

The ewes are led to wonder how
those crows are said to be so bright?
They've no more cunning than a cow
to flock a field that shows such blight.

The crows, in turn, cry raucous glee
for plough has shaved away the stubble.
They pose intent upon their tree,
their eyes on worms throughout the rubble.

The field proves this uneasy pairing:
whatever green it grows it owes
to worms below, whose active casting
enriches soil for feed, and crows.

Falling Up

Sophie Blanchard was the world's
first balloon aviatrix (1778-1819).

So like Icarus, wanting more,
Madame Sophie Blanchard, ascendant,
never content simply to achieve
that freedom so many seek,

but gloriously intent to exceed
her limits and go beyond
what had been already grasped,
by reaching for the next delight.

She failed, yet while falling
onto the unforgiving ground
sparks from her fierce descent
ignite the flames of inspiration

for those whose later, bolder leaps,
thrusting hard against our earthly chains,
hoped to forge still higher aims—
knowing those, too, would be shattered.

Homeboy

Maybe I bag your groceries,
maybe I clean your pool,
maybe I trim your hedges,
but I'm no fool.

Maybe I lack the fashion,
maybe I've torn my jeans,
maybe I need a haircut,
but I've got dreams.

Maybe we're not on welfare,
Mom and Sis and Bro,
maybe my daddy's long gone,
maybe you don't know.

Maybe my skin isn't just like yours,
maybe my teeth aren't white,
maybe your so-called standards
aren't altogether right.

Maybe I'd work very hard to win,
maybe I'd learn from a book,
maybe my abilities
are worth another look.

Vigil

The grey elephant stands waiting
on an old green window-shade mural
stretched across the wall above the bed.
Flakes from his poster-painted hide
drift down upon the narrow mattress.

The palm tree jungle that surrounds him
has lost half its fronds and coconuts,
and the dulled rays of a tropical sun
are eclipsed by dusty window light
seeping through limp curtains.

Wallpaper parrots compete for space
with pennants and yellowed posters,
while tarnished trophies stand sentinel
amid model cars and baseball mitts
beside a closet filled with memories,

where worn jerseys in team colors
hang like faded battle banners
above a mound of battered cleats.
The grey elephant waits patiently.
On the dresser, a folded flag.

Mentors

I've heard and learned your words, my Da,
and dwelled on them for years,
we must not bow to boots and brass
and dare not show them fear.

I've sat your sermons, monsignor,
and prayed on them full well,
I've learned about ungodly men
and know they're doomed to hell.

I've slept through many classes, Sir,
and bent to learn your cane,
our honour and our heritage
take force to claim again.

I've sworn my oath with you, my lads,
and learned to strike and run,
you've taught me use of stones and fire
and justice by the gun.

I know to hate outsiders,
to act as all were foe,
accepted all your teachings:
now, however shall I go?

Cold Call

That day I was intent on making a good first impression:
new coat and tie, shoes shined, dressed for success.
When the call came I wondered who could have found me
standing there beside that executive secretary's desk?
Reaching for the phone, trying to look unsurprised,
as though calls came for me every day, anywhere,
I scarcely heard the voice, hollow and thin,
with that hiss long distance calls had back then.

It had been sudden, with little forewarning,
and no preparation by any of us. He'd felt
something more serious than indigestion,
enhanced by those arm and shoulder pains
common to so many laboring men.
I think I'll go down the street and see the doc,
is what my mother reported he'd said
as he pushed back from the table.

They'd found him sitting on the doctor's porch,
already gone, reluctant to disturb another dinnertime.
What had it been like for my mother, I've wondered,
waiting alone at that table for his return?
They tracked me down the next afternoon
waiting my turn in someone's fine office,
this only son, so eager to make good,
hoping to leave a lasting impression.

Father's Day

My father's grave is under water
off in the corner of Oak Hill cemetery,
fed by a spring no one remarked
the day they dug him in.

Sheets of drab green canvas
secured our perimeter, as ribboned veterans
shot the volley and blew the Taps
and folded the flag for my mother to hold.

Today my knees are soaked clear through,
wet as my cheeks, as I work to clean
the moss and rust from his headstone.
Fire, not water, was his element;

war smoldered on within him,
an incendiary round gone astray
to flare hot, unpredictable, consuming
any of us who got too close.

Perhaps this lush wet field has finally
drowned his rage, the solace of water
cleansing like tide on Pacific beaches
spreads its wash to cover silent sands.

Hometown

A Main Street town,
a pom-pom marching band high school town,
a downtown drugstore hangout town
for the kids growing up, the kids hanging on.

A Greyhound bus flag-stop town:
plenty of departures, few returns.
Cash flow, job flow, empty families,
ghost storefronts and shuttered houses,
holes in roofs and in the streets.

They say you can't go home again.
Who would?

Fields behind our house
once endless rows of corn
now grow smokestacks.
Grey soot falls on headstones
marking my parents' graves.

Wet black road at dusk
points away past empty houses.
Weeds stand in rotting snow.

Winter wanes but does not thaw
this ice around my heart.

Plums

The doe stands poised and still, one breath from flight,
prepared to turn and bolt into the night;
then dips her slender neck, so gracefully,
and lips the fallen plums beneath the tree.

Though lights from passing cars flick through the leaves
to dapple her smooth hide, she hides with ease,
but haunches tense when breeze brings scent of man—
she lifts her head, and drops it down again.

As she resumes her graze, her instincts true,
she lays her claim upon the fruit anew
and takes her fill of plums upon the ground,
then stands erect to work the tree around.

Unmoved by man's control of his domain
the doe moves on. Few plums remain.

Dichotomy

Early, when I walk the dog,
I leash him tight and pay him out
down the pathway toward the gate.

Ducking scrappy shrubs I flinch
the moment that I feel the touch
of sudden web against my face.

Though the dog strains onward hard
I twist and try to brush the cling,
senses tensed for subtle crawl.

As I clench and pull to set his lead
I scrub at skin to ward my fear—
both hands intent to claim control.

The Day My Dog Died

The day my dog died he was waiting
to greet me with the slight heartbeat of his tail
at the foot of the stairs he could no longer climb.

The day my dog died I took him outside
into the yard and witnessed his shame
at his inability to walk or even lift a leg.

The day my dog died I spread a blanket
upon the floor of the examining room
and sat with his head cradled in my arms,

and watched the dullness grow within his eyes
as one leg twitched, and his gaunt chest sighed,
and he gave up his dream of catching the yellow cat.

Hiatus

The house is still, an unexpected hush,
no more alarms, excited barks; no rush
from front to back to front, and then once more
the skid of nails, the clamor at the door:
all done. This quietness unbroken now,
and yet I sense her presence near, somehow.
Nothing has filled that space, nor in my heart;
who'd have thought an old dog's graceless art
to bark and run and sleep and beg and kiss
is something I could treasure, or would miss?

Deliberation

Forward by small shuffles
he shoves his scaffolding,
its legs scraping at the shine
past nurses gossiping in their station.

Pursuing cracks in worn linoleum
as though led by a gas station map
he counts each familiar step
from ward to hallway washroom

where privacy eludes his grasp
with a door intended not to latch
and flickering fluorescent lights
buzz like flies in a privy long gone.

He sits to bend and strain again
against his limitations,
and hopes for a quick release
from this uncertainty.

Mirror Image

Who is this stranger in my bathroom mirror—
the ghost of an ancestor? If only he were clearer.
Where are my specs? Damned things are never there,
but wait, they rest above, perched in my hair.
What hair? Don't mock my shining pate,
premature loss has always been my fate,
and hair's not the only thing to disappear:
I haven't had my manhood up at all this year,
although I'd never know, below this gut,
when conditions might be ready for a rut.
Thank goodness I've been spared the chance
of medical emergency, should I attempt that dance.
Yet I surely grudge the possibility I'd meet
a cute responder, who'd sweep me off my feet.
Come to think, I'd no doubt be splayed already:
even at the best of times I'm none too steady,
and such an opportunity to spread my bony knees
would be lost, in circumstances sure to seize
this worn heart, which thank goodness still provides
that essential spark, and keeps my hopes alive.

Reflection

mirror playing tricks
pretends I am left-handed
pretends I am old

Taylor's Pond, Cape Cod

Dog Days

A clutter of rowboats beached belly-up like a litter of pups
dozes in the heat of this August day,
waiting for someone to whistle them into the water.

One sleek kayak nosing out the channel
slips carefully through rushes, alert
for something to flush. Insects hang heavy.

Working breeds, staked offshore,
bob and tug at their restraints,
eager to be off and running up-pond.

September

The pond, mirror still, is alive with possibility.
Suddenly a silvered fish breaks to take an insect.
A spiraling osprey makes her triumphant plunge.
Neither can survive the other's element,
yet this brief transaction is their key to life.

Almanac

This morning a swatch of reddened maple leaves
flares along one low limb. A vee of geese
focuses in the crisp lens of the pond.
I see my breath and shrug my jacket close.
Today will be shorter than the last.

Lowering

Clumps of cold mist drift over grey water,
wrap their gauze around shore birds seeking forage.

Late-bloomed rugosa leak blots of crimson
high on the bank above scraping marsh grasses.
A boat, tarped tight, rocks at its mooring.
Seaward a low horn groans through the fog.

Balance

Morning fog brings clarity to my purpose.
It's time to lay back the rose canes
and prepare the winter bedding.

Trees no longer hide the sky's bleak message
written on the leaves that drift around me.
Their colors cannot disguise their failed ambitions.

Yet, for every leaf that I regret
a child may clap his hands and shout
Look!

Soulcatcher

Some cultures believe
a photograph
will steal your soul.

My box of faded images
works this magic
in reverse.

Thus I rediscover
who I was,
how alive

we were,
how bereft
we have become.

Machismo

*(Craig Breedlove, a five-time land speed
record holder, was the first to reach
400mph, then 500mph, and 600mph.)*

Craig topped 408 on the Salt Flats in 1963,
the year I first made the earth move.

He was stroking 600 by '65
and I was just hitting my stride.

By 2013 he aimed to double his score
with the help of science and another driver.

I'll settle for a little quiver, some air
in my lungs, still standing erect.

September's Child

Born on the autumnal equinox
I've straddled both seasons,
attuned to summer's heat
while frost invades my years.

During the brief anniversary
I pause to catch my breath
as memories of sun-shined days
drift and melt away.

The celestial clock won't hesitate:
in just another heartbeat
I'll resume my measured tilt
away from day toward night.

Countdown

Shoulder season, Summer's orphan, left behind
along with litter from the Labor Day sales,
marking time until the equinox clocks you out.

Most of us believe you've already gone,
headed for the antipodes on a fast freighter
loaded with dark glasses and skimpy swimsuits.

It's no wonder you think you've been forgotten,
waiting in traffic all these recent mornings
behind the flashing red lights of loaded school buses

while the sun's still hot enough to raise blisters.
Let's head for that seafood restaurant on the beach
where we'll finally be able to get a table right away.

We'll order one last gin and tonic and a bucket of clams
before they stack the chairs and put up the shutters
and you realize it's time to take off for your next gig.

Road Trip

Driving out to meet old friends for lunch
we aim for a restaurant not too far away,
chosen for access, safety, and clean restrooms.
Caution is the name of the game nowadays.

This late-formed mastery of tethered driving
belies earlier belief in roads that never ended
where no trip was too long, every destination ours,
and immortality rode in the seat beside us.

Patchwork

Late in our marriage I built a room,
piecing it from fitted boards to cover up
the walls of a porch beginning to lean.
Though slightly slant and often hotter
or colder than we'd have liked,
it made a pretty place, surfaced
with textured grain and an elegant finish,
cozy like a small boat's cabin.

It suited our needs in a house grown old,
a dwelling where we learned which doors
would stick without warning, which windows,
increasingly opaque, offered distorted views.
I'd become skilled at papering over cracks,
restoring the face of surfaces gone wrong,
hiding ills beyond repair that lay beneath.

My father showed me how to fix a house.
He led by example; as a boy I carried boards
while he sawed and pounded and cursed.
His techniques were his own invention
and I learned the heart of his philosophy:
that nothing acquired is ever easily let go,
that we are well served by patching over,
that we must make it up as we go along.

James **Broschart** grew up in the hard coal region of the Appalachian Mountains in Pennsylvania, graduated from St. John's College in Annapolis, and studied poetry with Elliott Coleman in the Johns Hopkins Writing Seminars. He has retired from several occupations, including college teaching, public television production, technical writing, and bookstore management. He has written about lifelong learning, safe schools, and marine science for various federal agencies. He taught English composition to sailors aboard the aircraft carrier *U.S.S. Independence* and developed emergency management manuals for Department of Energy nuclear sites.

James resides in southwest Virginia in the midst of the Blue Ridge Mountains with his wife Kay. Retirement has provided him with the opportunity to turn back to poetry. Having lived through fourteen U.S. presidents he is eager to see what will happen next. He can be reached at brolink1@hotmail.com and on Facebook.

www.ingramcontent.com/pod-product-compliance
Lightning Source LLC
Chambersburg PA
CBHW021203090426
42740CB00008B/1215